LIGHTNING BOLT BOOKS™

What Is MONEY, Anyway?

Why Dollars and Coins Have Value

Jennifer S. Larson

Lerner Publications Company

Minneapolis

For my husband, Michael, who shares his money with me.

Lerner Publications Company
A division of Lerner Publishing Group, Inc.
241 First Avenue North
Minneapolis, MN 55401 U.S.A.

Website address: www.lernerbooks.com

Library of Congress Cataloging-in-Publication Data

Larson, Jennifer S., 1967–
        What is money, anyway? : why dollars and coins have value / by Jennifer S. Larson.
            p.   cm. — (Lightning bolt books™—Exploring economics)
        Includes index.
        ISBN 978-0-7613-3915-1 (lib. bdg. : alk. paper)
        1. Money—Juvenile literature. 2. Money—United States—Juvenile literature. I. Title.
    HG221.5.L37 2010
        332.4—dc22   2009027469

Manufactured in the United States of America
1 — BP — 12/15/09

Contents

Money

Look! Someone dropped a piece of paper on the sidewalk.

That's not just any paper.
That's money!

Our money is made of metal and paper. In the past, people used stones, beads, and other things for money.

Native Americans used beads called wampum as money.

We use dollars and cents in the United States.

Coins and Bills

These are U.S. coins. Each one is worth a certain amount.

How much is each of these coins worth?

A penny is worth one cent.

A nickel is worth five cents.

A dime is worth ten cents.

A quarter is worth twenty-five cents.

9

Here is a dollar bill and
some dollar coins. A dollar
equals one hundred cents.

Bills also come in five dollars and ten dollars. And they come in twenty dollars, fifty dollars, and one hundred dollars.

How Is Money Made?

The U.S. government makes our money. Coins are made at a special factory. It's called the U.S. Mint.

Coins are made in this building.

U.S. bills are made at a place with a long name. **It's the Bureau of Engraving and Printing.**

This worker is checking some newly printed dollar bills.

Most dollar bills wear out
in about two years. The
old bills are shredded. Workers
make new bills to replace them.

Coins last longer than bills. But sometimes coins need to be replaced. Old coins are melted down to make new ones.

These coin blanks will be stamped to make new coins.

Let's Trade

What is so special about money? It's just paper and metal, right?

What makes money special is how we use it. We can trade money for things we want and need.

Money can be traded for food at the grocery store.

People use money to buy goods and services. Goods are things we eat, wear, and use. Services are work that people do for others.

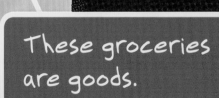

These groceries are goods.

Sometimes people trade for what they want. They exchange one good or service for another good or service.

People trade goods at swap meets.

You might trade with a friend.
Maybe you have a cookie.
Your friend has an ice cream
cone. You decide to swap.
Is that a fair trade?

These kids are
trading toys.

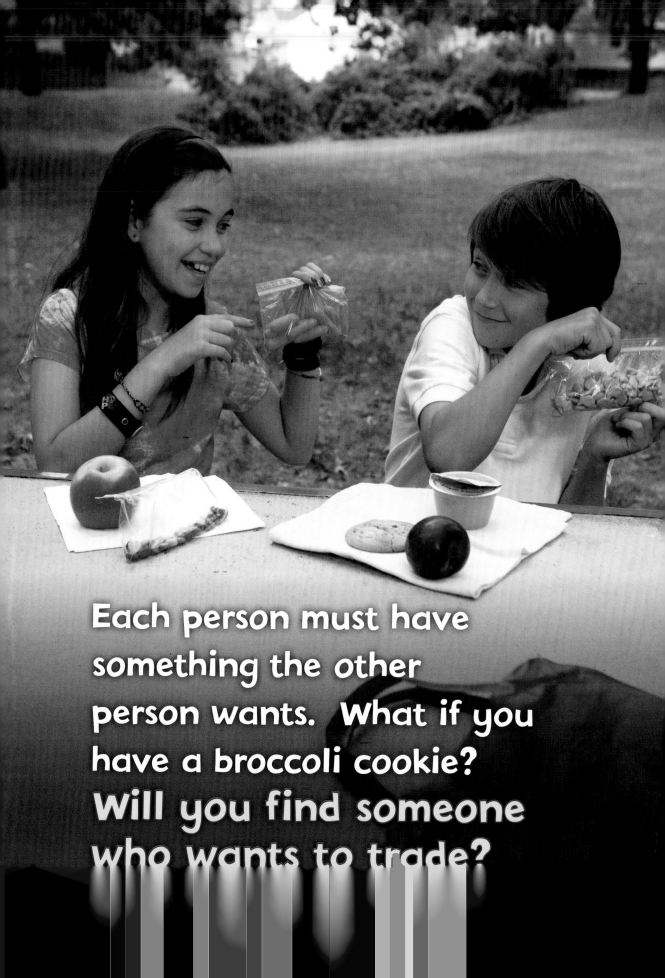

Each person must have
something the other
person wants. What if you
have a broccoli cookie?
Will you find someone
who wants to trade?

Both people expect to be happy after they trade.

These boys are happy with the baseball cards they ended up with after a trade.

Money Makes It Easier

Most of the time, people trade money for goods and services. Money makes trading easier.

This man did work on the other man's house in exchange for money.

Let's say your friend pays you for your cookie. Now you can buy the ice cream cone you want. Or maybe you will buy a toy.

How much does this bread cost?
The price is the amount of
money we pay for something.

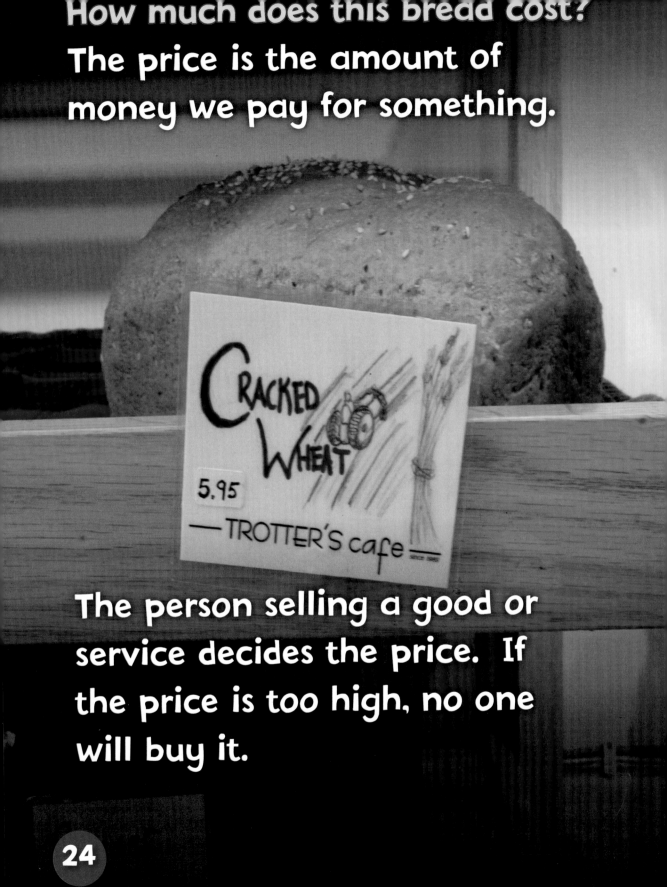

The person selling a good or
service decides the price. If
the price is too high, no one
will buy it.

If the price is too low, the seller will not earn enough money. She will not be able to buy flour to make more bread.

A seller has to make enough money from her product to make more to sell.

A market is anyplace where people buy or sell goods and services. Several people might be selling cookies in a market. That gives people choices.

Markets give people a choice of what to buy.

Which cookie tastes better? Which one costs less?

What will you buy with your money?

Activity
Design a Coin

Artists create the pictures we see on bills and coins. Pretend the U.S. president has asked *you* to design a new coin. Will you design a penny, nickel, dime, quarter, half-dollar, or dollar coin? Draw your new coin on a sheet of paper.

Coins often include pictures of buildings, people, and animals.

Fun Facts

- The Chinese were the first people to use paper money. The Chinese government printed an early form of money more than one thousand years ago.

- In Ethiopia, people once used salt as money. They traded bars of hard salt called rock salt. The same salt was also used for cooking!

- Modern U.S. bills are printed on special paper. That paper contains cotton fibers. The cotton makes the bills last longer.

- Who was the first African American to be pictured on a U.S. coin? Booker T. Washington! A half dollar named for him was made from 1946 to 1951.

- In 1999, the U.S. Mint began making state quarters. Each new quarter is named for a U.S. state. The first was the Delaware state quarter. The last was the Hawaii state quarter. It was made in 2008.

Glossary

bill: a piece of paper money

cent: a unit of U.S. money. One hundred cents equals one dollar.

coin: a piece of metal money

dollar: the main unit of U.S. money. A dollar is worth one hundred cents.

good: a thing you can touch that can be bought and sold

market: a place where people buy or sell goods and services

price: the amount of money we pay for something

service: work done by people for others

trade: to exchange one thing for another

Further Reading

Doudna, Kelly. *Let's Add Coins*. Edina, MN: Abdo, 2003.

Enchanted Learning: Money and Coins
http://www.enchantedlearning.com/themes/money
.shtml

H.I.P. Pocket Change
http://www.usmint.gov/kids

Larson, Jennifer S. *What Can You Do with Money?*: *Earning, Spending, and Saving*. Minneapolis: Lerner Publications Company, 2010.

Roberson, Erin. *All About Money*. New York: Children's Press, 2004.

Index

Photo Acknowledgments

The images in this book are used with the permission of: © Todd Strand/Independent
Picture Service, pp. 2, 4, 5, 9 (all), 10 (top), 19, 20, 21, 23, 24, 27, 28; © MPI/Hulton
Archive/Getty Images, p. 6; © Brie Cohen/Independent Picture Service, pp. 7, 11, 30;
© iStockphoto.com/Philip Dyer, p. 8; © iStockphoto.com/Juanmonino, p. 10 (bottom);
© iStockphoto.com/smithcjb, p. 12; © Rob Crandall/The Image Works, p. 13;
© iStockphoto.com/Joe Cicak, p. 14; © Justin Sullivan/Getty Images, p. 15;
© iStockphoto.com/monkeybusinessimages, p. 16; © iStockphoto.com/Edyta
Pawlowska, p. 17; © Douglas Peebles Photography/Alamy, p. 18; © David Sacks/Lifesize/
Getty Images, p. 22; © Anderson Ross/Blend Images/Getty Images, p. 25; © Walter
Bibikow/Photolibrary, p. 26; © iStockphoto.com/John Sfondilias, p. 28 (left);
Smithsonian Institution, National Numismatic Collection, p. 29; © iStockphoto.com/
Skip O'Donnell, p.31.

Front cover: © Tommy Flynn/Photonica/Gettyimages.com (top); © Matt Gray/
Photolibrary.com